Dominance & Submission

The Art, The Act & The Pleasure of Erotic Play

Introduction

I'm in a 24/7 with my Master, we're supposed to attend a black sheet party in a dungeon after a munch on a downtown bar. He's into golden showers but scat play is my hard limit. Those vanillas don't know what they're missing.

The words above may confuse you but to the initiated, the words make complete sense and make for an interesting evening.

Dominance and submission, these words evoke images of not only pleasure, arousal and climax but also leather, pain and extreme sexual acts. It is as much a cause of erotic fantasies as they are a reason for wild curiosities. Once a taboo, this unique sexual arrangement is gaining recognition and even popularity. Still, much of this sexual art is either misunderstood or still unknown to the majority.

Whether it is a fantasy, curiosity or both, this book will satisfy any secret needs for this kind of information. Do you want to know the origins of this practice? Do you want to be familiar with the vocabulary, terminology and lingo used by practitioners? Do you want to know the many dominance and submission relationships styles? Are you interested in how practitioners come into agreement on their plays? Do you want a list and detailed descriptions of the equipment and safety involved? Do you have other questions that you may be afraid or even embarrassed to ask?

This book will give you a brief history dominance and submission as part of the BDSM culture. A list of private words used by practitioners is also added along with their meanings. Included also are detailed discussion on various relationship styles and the equipment used during the plays. Added are concepts of consent, safety and a list of FAQs.

Discover the secret world of this sexual art. Satisfy your curiosity. Unravel the art, the act and the pleasure of erotic play. Are you a Dom, a sub or a switch? Read on and find out.

information is without contract or any type of guarantee assurance.

The trademarks that are used are without any consent, and the publication of the trademark is without permission or backing by the trademark owner. All trademarks and brands within this book are for clarifying purposes only and are the owned by the owners themselves, not affiliated with this document.

Table of Contents

Chapter One: Brief History

The terms dominance and submission were first recorded at around 1969. It is believed to be the term used to refer to the middle ground between the erotic practices of bondage, discipline, submission and masochism or BDSM. On the extreme left is the practice for bondage and discipline and on the extreme right is the practice for sadism and masochism. In the middle of these extremes are domination and submission.

Dominance and submission may seem to be gaining ground recently; however, its roots can be traced as far back as the 9th century. Ancient Spartan religious practices involved the ritual flagellation of young adolescent men by the priestesses of the temple. Aside from these written record, the first ever image of BDSM was dated at around the 5th century. This time it was an Italian fresco of a two men who flagellate a woman with a cane during intercourse. Around the 4th century, journals were found that give stories of males and females who ask to be bound and then whipped as foreplay.

Indian culture also has its share of in the history of domination and submission. In the Kama Sutra, texts provide instructions on the use of different ways of hitting during intercourse. Each technique is meant to elicit various pleasurable cries of pain. Aside from hitting, there will be pinching, biting and scratching.

Fast forward to the early 1900s, three sources are credited to be the foundations of the modern erotic practices: American Fetish, European Fetish and Gay Leather. Augmenting these sources are the various sexual games that were played in brothels across the Western world.

After the internet was introduced, secret practitioners found a way to connect anonymously with those who shared their preferences. It paved the way for building local networks, access to information and purchase of equipment. It also allowed for other expressions of pleasure. Even without physical contact, persons with this sexual preference can text, email, chat, call and video call their partners.

Today, dominance and submission are defined as the erotic practices that take pleasure through either giving or receiving control through the use of customs, rituals and equipment. Once considered taboo, this erotic lifestyle has exploded into popular culture.

More and more individuals are becoming more open about their practices, such as the formation of the Leather Movement and BDSM clubs all over the world. The practices also gained legal recognition from various countries. For example Austria, Canada, Germany, Sweden and Switzerland will not prosecute any injury done if under the consent of the recipient. Italy, the United Kingdom and the United States criminalize certain practices. However, none can the dispute the exposure and popularity that the community enjoys now.

Chapter Two: Terminology

Over the course of its history, practitioners of the art have developed their own vocabulary or lingo. Their terminology is an expression of their identity and community. Interest in this sexual behavior often begins with a familiarity of the words used.

Below are few of the many words used by those in the community. The list below is meant to give you with a working knowledge for future references.

#

24/7: Refers to a relationship where all rules, behaviors and practices are expected to be followed continuously. Certain dominance and submission relationships assume the roles only during sex. In a 24/7, the roles persist regardless of time and place.

A

Animal transformation: This is usually the fantasy of a submissive to assume the role of an animal in the relationship. He may be a dog that is collared or a horse that is mounted. Animal play is the term used when the submissive behaves and dresses similarly to his animal transformation.

Aftercare: This is the time when the partners talk about their experience after an intercourse. This where they can talk about what they liked or disliked about the behaviors their partner need. For those without a 24/7 relationship, this is important to bring them outside the fantasy and back to reality.

Ageplay: This a relationship when a dominant assumes adult authority figures in the play. For example, it can be a parent to a child, a teacher to a student or a police to a juvenile delinquent.

Auctioned off: This is a scenario when a dominant person acts as an auctioneer. He then sells his submissive partner as a slave.

B

Bad pain: This is a type of pain that is beyond the consent or desire of the partner. This is outside you or your partner's pain thresholds. The opposite of this is good pain, which provides sensual pleasure or consented levels of pain.

Black sheet party: This refers to an orgy for BDSM.

Bondage: This is the restraint done to a partner; it can be total restraint involving the entire body for example in a sling or a specific part of the body such as in mouth, breast of other parts.

Bottom: This a person who is the receiver of the sexual actions performed by a top. The top is the doer while the bottom is the one that is being done.

Breath control: This is when a dominant controls the breathing of the submissive, often by grasping the neck.

Butt plug: This is a toy that is meant to be inserted into the anal cavity similar to a dildo. However, it has a base that is flared to prevent it from getting inserted all the way. Some butt plugs can vibrate.

C

Chastity: This is a relationship where the dominant prevents his partner to achieving any genital arousal or orgasm from taking place. The submissive release and climax are at the mercies of the whims of the dominant. The dominant keeps his partner in constant arousal and delays resolution. This denial is achieved through the use of chastity belts for females and a cock cage for men.

CBT: This is an acronym for cock and ball torture. This is the painful stimulation of the male genitals which creates pleasure. Genitorture is a general term.

Collared: This is a status of a submissive when owned by a dominant. A collared by may be shared or exclusively owned by a master. The ceremony of the acceptance of a dominant to a submissive is called a collaring.

Consent: This is the terms of reference or rules of the relationship.

Consensual non-consensuality: This is the agreement between partners who share a great deal of trust. The terms or scenario are usually unknown so as to surprise the partner in the upcoming session.

Contract: This is the written document that contains all rules, roles, expectations and limitations. It is not legally binding.

D

DM: This is the initials for a Dungeon Master. Their role is to keep the session within its limits and at the same time encourage participants to perform. Simply speaking a DM is both the referee and cheer leader for the session.

Dominant: This is the person in the relationship that has control. Alternative terms are Dom and D. The female D is also called a Domme. The term dominatrix is rarely used.

Dungeon: This is the area where BDSM sessions occur and doubles as storage or display for the BDSM equipment.

E

Edgeplay: This is a play that is reflective of a potential of harm. The greater the risk, the more pleasurable it becomes for one or both of the persons involved. For example, it can be breathing control involving near strangulation of a submissive.

Electro-play: This is another play that makes use of electrical stimulation.

F

Fetish: This is an object or situation that creates pleasure or arousal. For example, it can be kissing the toes or the sight of armpits.

Figging: This is the insertion of ginger in the vagina or anal cavity.

Fire play: This is a play that makes use of fire for the heat it causes in the bottom's skin. This is often achieved by blowing a light torch, cotton or a pool of fuel towards the submissive.

Fisting: This is the insertion of the entire hand into anal cavity or vagina.

G

Golden showers: This is the play of urinating on or being urinated upon a person.

Gunplay: This is a play making use of real and fake guns.

H

Handkerchief codes: Worn on the left means the wearer is a top, right is a bottom.

Hard limits: This is the threshold of a person, actions or behaviors that will not be done regardless of the partner or situation.

Harem: This is a group of subs or bottoms.

Hogtie: This is the physical restraining of a submissive, starting on their wrist and ankles. Both ties are then fastened together behind the sub's back.

I

Impact play: This is a play that involves hitting through the use of paddles, whips, rods and other equipment.

Infantilism: This is a play where the dominant is a parent or any adult role and the submissive is a child or baby.

K

Knife play: This is a play where the edge of knife is used to gently caress the submissive's skin, without actually cutting.

M

Masochism: The experience of pleasure when feeling pain. The person who feels pleasure on this pain is the masochist.

Mummification: This is a play involving total restraint by covering the entire body with a thin plastic sheet. Only the mouth and nose are exposed so the submissive can breathe.

Munch: This is a group of people who are into BDSM but visit a non-BDSM club or gathering. They often go there wearing average clothes instead of their usual leather outfits.

N

Needle play: This is a play involving temporary piercings during a session.

Nyotaimori: This is a submissive lying naked in a table with sushi pieces spread all over his body.

P

Painslut: This is a person who specifically takes pleasure in pain but not general submissive practices.

Pegging: This is a play when a dominant female wears a dildo then penetrates her male partner's anus.

Play party: This is a venue involving several BDSM sessions of different varieties or plays.

ProDom: A paid professional dominant. A female can also be called a ProDomme.

Ponyboy: This is a play where the submissive is wearing a pony costume, complete with a mouth bit and a tail that is attached to an anal plug.

Pup-play: This is a play where the submissive acts like a dog. He accepts orders from his human master to bark, to eat or to drink in a bowl and other submissive actions.

R

Rape play: This is a play where rape is simulated. A sub acts as a victim in resisting the sexual assault and a Dom is the rapist.

S

Sadism: The experience of inflicting pain that causes pleasure. The person is the sadist.

SSC: This is an acronym for safe, safe and consensual. This is the criteria used by BDSM to evaluate an appropriate BDSM contract.

Safeword: This is a word that is agreed upon by both Dom and sub. The sub is meant to give this word as a signal for the Dom to stop.

Scat play: This is a play where feces are used.

Scene: This is a session of BDSM.

Slave: This is another term for a sub.

Soft limits: This is in contrast to hard limits. These are actions or behaviors that someone is willing to negotiate in performing.

Subdrop: This is the experience of a sub of flu-like symptoms. It normally occurs after a BDSM session that causes an endorphin rush.

Subspace: This refers to the state of a mind of a sub during an endorphin rush.

Switch: This is a person who takes pleasure in both being a Dom or a sub.

T

Tit torture: This is a play that involves inflicting pain on the breasts and nipples.

TNG: This is an acronym for The Next Generation. This is a group of people who prefers sessions with younger BDSM practitioners, often belonging to 18 to 35 age range.

Top: The doer of the action, he is not necessarily a Dom since the Dom can be the director of the session and order the sub to top him.

Topping from the bottom: A bottom that claims to be submissive but really prefers to be on top.

TPE: This is an acronym for total power exchange. This is a relationship that surrenders total control of a sub's life to a Dom.

V

Vanilla: This is a non-BDSM practitioner and also the term called for sexual activities that are non-BDSM.

W

Warm-up: This is the foreplay to a BDSM scene.

WIITWD: This is an acronym for what it is that we do, this is the term used for describing all sexual practices.

Wax play: This is a play making using hot candle wax. It is often allowed to drip in the sub's body.

Chapter Three: Relationship Styles

There are various activities involved between a Dom and a sub. This is made possible by the almost countless combinations between the partners' preferences, fetishes and fantasies. Add to this variety are the tools used in the play.

There are generally three categories of relationship styles:

1. Play. This relationship is the expression of sexual preferences under specific scenarios. This is when parties engage inside different dungeons (place), spanning different sessions (timeframe) and performing different scenes (roles or storylines). It is called playing because it is temporary, when the session is up or the scene has ended, the BDSM relationship is terminated.

2. Professional. This relationship is similar to play except that at least one party is hired and paid for his services. Offers include the performance of several scenes in various sessions. Both Doms and the rare subs and all genders can be a professional. They often work in an affiliated dungeon.

3. Long term. This relationship is distinctly different because it is characterized by extended sessions. This is generally the case for committed partners who found a near perfect match with another in terms of their sexual preferences. This relationship was once considered impossible because it was thought to be possible only for those who are married or with strong partnerships. However, recent studies show that this relationship is indeed possible even outside marriage.

Here are some of the plays that range from the well-known to the rather unique:

1. Master & Maid

2. Sexual Denial

3. Humiliation

4. Human Furniture

5. Human Toilet

6. Animal Play

7. Feminization

8. Infantilism

9. Fetishes

Master & Maid

In this play, the Dom assumes the role of the master and the sub acts as a maid, servant, housekeeper, servant or even a slave. There is no racial discrimination or any cultural sensitivity in this scene, there is only sex, pleasure and eroticism. Gender roles are also disregarded here; a man can be a slave to a woman, especially if the relationship is between a Domme and a male sub.

A play can begin with a Master ordering his maid to clean his toys, sweep the dungeon and order her to do other menial tasks. The Master can then advance to more sexually suggestive acts such as ordering the sub to undress him, undress her and start to perform sexual acts. A Master will also feign disappointment on a task and punish the maid. He may then make use of whips to inflict pain or restrain her to cause discomfort.

Sexual Denial

In this play, the male sub will be forced to wear a cock cage. The Dom will then top him by pleasuring him in several ways. However, once the sub is nearing orgasm, the Dom will withhold the stimulation. She may stop with the pleasuring altogether and replace it with various neutral acts that do not cause any sexual pleasure. She may even stop the play altogether. Once the arousal is about to subside, she will then pleasure the sub again.

This cycle is repeated over and over again. The sub will then beg the Dom to unlock the cock cage and allow him to reach orgasm. The Dom receives pleasure from having power of the sub's sexual satisfaction while the sub also takes pleasure from his sexual denial.

Humiliation

In this play, the Dom will be creating the illusion of abuse to the sub in different ways. The sub may be required to undress in front of several people. She may be required to expose herself or her genitals in various embarrassing positions. She can also be seemingly forced to do sexual acts that may be degrading to her, such as giving oral or receiving anal sex. The Dom can also simulate sexual assault or rape. She may also be verbally abused through various profanities and insults.

Human Furniture

This play often involves several subs catering to one or few Doms. Usually, the subs are naked and assume several positions that imitate common furniture. A sub can assume a crawl position and the Dom can sit on her back. By raising her back, the sub can also become a coffee table with the Dom putting his feet on the table.

Human Toilet

An extension of the human furniture play, the Dom will pretend to need to go to the toilet to relieve him. Instead of urinating on a real toilet, the Dom will urinate on a sub. The sub can take various positions such as lying down with the Dom standing above her and then urinating. More risky practices involve urinating directly on the mouth, vagina and anal cavity.

Animal Play

In this play, the Dom can choose to have a sub that is a dog, pony, cat or any other animal. A dog can then be leashed and the Dom will act as if he is walking her on the dungeon. He will then feed or let her drink in a bowl. If the sub is pony, a bit gag is usually used with a harness attached to it. The Dom can then ride the pony around the dungeon.

Feminization

In this play, the sub is usually a male who assume a female role. He will be cross dressing and acting in female behaviors. The Dom can either be a male or female who will treat the male as a female. In sexual intercourse, if the Dom is a female, she will be wearing a penis strap attached to her genital area or called as pegging.

Infantilism

In this play, the sub assumes the role of an infant. He may be naked or wear infant clothes and accessories, such as diapers, bibs or pacifiers. The Dom can do everything from taking care of the baby by feeding, bathing or changing the diapers. The infant can also soil himself, which later will be cleaned by the Dom. Part of the play, can also involve the baby doing something bad. The Dom must then punish the sub through some form of consequences often involving spanking.

Fetishes

Instead of being plays themselves, most fetishes are part of a larger play. The object or situation that is the unique fetish of the practitioner takes center stage in the play. Fetishes involve a specific object or situation that arouses a person sexually. There are various types of fetishes that serve to intensify the sensual pleasures of a fetishist.

Highly associated with dominance and submission fetishes are:

1. Clothing and materials, these include leather, latex and rubber that are used for, uniforms, boots, skirts, gloves, bracelets, collars and other accessories.

2. Background and personality profiles, these include attraction to people who are heavy, elderly, children, transgender, and disabled or have amputated body parts and criminals.

3. Body fluids and wastes, these include blood, menses, feces, urine, vomit, mucus, saliva and semen.

4. Body parts, these include feet, armpits, noses, eyeballs, butt and hair.

5. Situations, these include inflicting, receiving or observing scenes such as pain, asphyxiation, rape, ingestion of flesh, being recorded during intercourse, robbed, other dangerous situations and seeing a partner having sex with another person. Exposure of the genitals in public can also create pleasure.

6. Roles, these include assuming the behaviors of the opposite sex, being an infant, vampire, wolf or other mythical beings.

There are certainly more fetishes that are not included in the list. There are also cases that one person may have more than one fetish. In the dominance and submission relationship, fetishes are used to enhance the play.

Chapter Four: Consent & Contract

Consent and contract take a special meaning in the world of dominance and submission. Consent is essentially the permission both parties give to each other in the expression of their sexuality. A contract is the written document that specifies and details the scope and limitations of the consent.

These concepts are highly misunderstood outside the world of BDSM; this is because of the various preferences, definition and acceptance of the art to outsiders. Some generally accepted practices between a Dom and a sub are considered illegal and criminal to others.

There are generally two concepts of consent: informed and contemporaneous. Informed consent is achieved when both parties are given complete information of the events that will happen in a BDSM session. If something is done outside of these details, there is no consent over that act. For example, a Dom and a sub agree that he will be using whips and rods to elicit pain. The sub agrees. During the course of the session, the Dom uses fire play, which is outside the agreed upon impact play. When a Dom uses fire play, he does not have the consent of the sub.

Contemporaneous consent gives the opportunity to both provide and rescind consent at any moment during the session. For example, both parties agree to both impact and fire play. When the Dom is about to blow fire to the sub's skin, the sub decides to rescind his consent by saying "stop" or "no." Based on this word alone, consent is rescinded and the previous agreed upon consent is null and void. This is a debatable subject in the BDSM world because it conflicts with some of the practices. For example, a sub cannot order a Dom or a slave cannot do anything outside her master's permission.

There are various kinds of consent that are agreed upon by both parties. Each is unique based on their preferences, scene, equipment and role play. However consent usually fall under three categories:

1. Temporary or short- term consent

2. Indefinite or long- term consent

3. Consensual non- consent

Temporary consent is the usual agreements between parties in dominance and submission relationships. These consent usually run for a couple of hours, overnight or the duration of the scene. The longer the session is, the more detailed the consent becomes. Often, detailed consents require a written and signed contract to signify agreement. Consent can have a few to several pages, especially for scenes that not only require long periods of time but also involving different plays and scenes.

Indefinite consent is rare and often made by parties who are in an equally long term relationship. This is because the preferences, fantasies, limitations and expectations of both partners are already known to each other. Most of these consents take the form of a slave contract. They are not legally binding but are used as the document for reference of the parties involved.

Rarer and even discouraged within the BDSM community is the consensual non-consent. This is a consent that assumes a perpetual and universal characteristic. It is often considered irrevocable between both partners and even without advanced information of what to expect in the BDSM relationship.

This type of consent requires total and complete trust between partners. Often, this consent is only between long time and committed partners. There is a huge risk for the safety, especially of the sub, because it gives the Dom permission to go beyond what is expected in the relationship.

There are three models or philosophies of consent:

1. SSC

2. RACK

3. PRICK

SSC stands for safe, sane and consensual. It encourages practitioners to determine and avoid health risks (safe). It also guides parties to perform every activity before, during and after the scene in full awareness, understanding and free from any mental incapacity (sane). Finally, all scenes must be done with full consent between the parties involved (consensual).

RACK stands for risk- aware or accepted consensual kink. It encourages those who accept this kind of consent to be knowledgeable on the risks of the scene (risk aware or accepted). With complete understanding of the risks involved, the parties agree and accept the risk assessment (consensual). The entire scene is defined as an alternative form of sexual expression (kink).

This consent contrasts with SSC because it believes nothing, including the practices, customs and behavior of BDSM practitioners, are completely safe. Instead, this consent encourages both parties to be aware and focused on the risk instead of the actual safety of the scene. This is because safety is a very subjective experience; a dangerous situation for some may be a pleasurable scene to another. Instead of safe and unsafe, there is only varying degrees of risk.

Finally PRICK stands for personal responsibility with informed consensual kink. This model suggests that each party is personally responsible for their individual actions. When they are able to accept the consequences, they can pursue their fantasies as long as both parties agree to it.

Take note that one practitioner does not necessarily have to follow only one kind of model in their consent. One or all three of the models can be used in different relationships. Most of the time, one person will use SSC to describe his BDSM philosophy to vanillas but use RACK with other members of the community.

Negotiation is the discussion of the terms of reference for the session, which when agreed upon, ultimately becomes the consent or the contract. Negotiation takes various processes. The processes are usually divided into two:

1. Formal. Negotiations of this kind take place before the scene. It is usually done between short termed or pick up partners. It can be done with paperwork, such as a checklist of the parties' hard and soft limits. There are structured discussions and documentations to create true understanding and acceptance. Commonly, an exhaustive battery of questions is asked to generate specific information instead of leaving vague areas in the scene. The BDSM community encourages this type of process.

2. Informal. This negotiation takes place while in the relationship or during the scene itself. It is a process of testing, respecting or even exceeding the limits of a partner during casual conversations, discussions and debates.

There are also several legal implications in the concept of consent. Most of the practices of dominance and submission, when viewed by an outsider, can be construed as assault, rape or other forms of criminal acts. There are varying precedents across different countries on the application of the consent. For example, a UK court arrested practitioners even when the play was under complete consent. On the other hand, a US court did not convict practitioners engaged in sodomy done in private. The court decided that sexual conduct done under consent was an expression of freedom and liberty.

Chapter Five: Restraints, Furniture, Stimulation & Dungeons

Dominance and submission are wildly recognized for the stereotypical whips used by Doms and collars worn by subs. These are only two of the many equipment and accessories used by practitioners.

Restraints

1. Cuffs, shackles and ropes. These are meant to tie the extremities either to an object or to another extremity. For example, a Dom can hogtie a sub using cuffs.

2. Ball, bit, inflatable and funnel gags. These are tied into the mouths of the sub. A ball is spherical while a bit is a rod-shaped gag. Inflatable or penis gags are to be inserted in the mouth for the sub to suck to arouse the Dom. Mouth guards are meant to prevent the sub from talking. Funnel gags are used to force a sub to ingest liquids.

3. Mittens, hoods, yokes, tapes and belts. These are bondage equipment that is meant to totally restrict the use of certain parts of the body. Mittens will prevent grasping; hoods will prevent seeing, yokes the movement of the arms and head, tapes for the mouth and belts for the body.

4. Chastity belts and cock rings. These are the accessories used to either deny arousal or delay orgasm. Chastity belts prevent the manipulation of the clitoris and the vagina of the females. Cock rings are worn around the base of the penis. It is used to sustain erection by keeping the blood in the penis. This also delays ejaculation. Another variation of the cock ring is a triple crown that can also restrict the testicles. This is meant to intensify the orgasm.

5. Clingfilm, strait jackets and sleep slacks. These provide total restraint for the entire body. The person is essentially mummified when Clingfilm is used.

6. Corsets, breast binders, cock cages and penis belt. These are meant to either enhance or restrict the sex organs. Corsets can raise the breasts making them look bigger. Penis belts restrain the erect penis in full display. Breast binders flatten the breast. Cock cages prevent full erection of the penis.

7. Collars. These are special accessories in the BDSM community. They are meant to indicate ownership of the wearer to a Dom. They come in a variety of shapes, colors and designs.

8. Humblers and spreader bars. Humblers are metal rods that are placed in between a man's thighs. In the middle of the rod is a slot where the scrotum can be inserted. It forces the wearer to keep the thighs apart because closing them in will squeeze the scrotum. To avoid the pain, the man keeps his thighs apart and his rectum exposed. The spreader bar works the same way but this time for a woman but without the scrotum slot.

Furniture

1. Racks, benches, frames, tables, chairs, stools and wheels. These are various surfaces where the sub can be restrained. They usually have slots to insert cuffs and other equipment. Racks and tables are meant to restrain a sub into a lying position, frames and benches to a position where the extremities are extended away from the body. Wheels rotate the body to an inverted position.

2. Hoists, slings and swings. These are meant to suspend the body midair. They can be calibrated so that the sub can be restrained in different positions. A person can be hoisted so that the genitals and other orifices are exposed.

3. St. Andrew's cross. This is a cross shaped like an X. The person is restrained with arms and legs stretched wide apart.

4. Queening stool or smotherbox. This is a special seat that allows facesitting. This is a sexual practice where one person sits on the face of his partner so that he can receive genital or anal stimulation through the partner's tongue.

Stimulation

1. Clamps. These are attached to the nipples of both women and men. It restricts blood flow thereby keeping them erect. The discomfort and pain induced can cause pleasure to the observer or the wearer.

2. Paddles, whips and floggers. These come in a variety of forms, materials and sizes. They are used for impact play.

3. Electrostimulation and automated machines. Electrostimulation are usually metallic dildos that allow electric current to pass through from the source to the genitals of the wearer. Automated machines range from simple to complex devices that can simulate intercourse to an actual person.

Two or more dungeons can be hosted in a BDSM party or club. These are venues where practitioners choose to congregate and meet other people with the same preferences. Various etiquette are observed in these clubs, some are strict by enforcing a dress code of leather, latex and other materials that exhibit the genitals and other secondary sex organs. Some are also more lenient, allowing vanillas to enter as voyeurs or exhibitionists.

The popularity of these clubs is because of several reasons. Most practitioners and their homes will not have access to a wide range of equipment or toys. There is also the issue of noise and privacy in a rather quiet neighborhood. Clubs solve these problems by providing a wide variety of toys, fully equipped dungeons and full expression of their sexual preferences in the comforts of the club.

Chapter Six: Safety

Safety takes a special notice in the sexual activity of BDSM practitioners. This goes beyond the use of contraceptives, such as condoms and other safe sex practices. Aside from the prevention of sexually transmitted diseases and unwanted pregnancies, actual physical harm is a risk for both the Dom and the sub.

In an ideal situation, both parties will engage in the play after thorough negotiations. Consent, whether verbal or written, is also given in advance. For those using SSC, RACK or PRICK, safety measures, risk awareness and personal accountabilities are already in place to create a safe environment. However, these ideal situations do not always occur prior to a play.

In a consensual non-consent model and a random pick up scenario, there are either unknown elements in the play or a mismatch in the preferences. There is also minimal or even no negotiation process done. These factors increase the risk of injury both physical and psychological to the parties involved.

There are various techniques used by the BDSM community to create a safer environment despite the lack of negotiations or more informed consent. Some of these are:

1. Safewords. These are previously agreed upon words that can be used to signal to a partner to stop the play. Different words can be used as long as they are not "no, don't or stop." Any words that are also associated with pain cannot be used "it hurts, ouch, etc." This is because these are words that are commonly used in plays or roles. A partner may not be able to distinguish between the role playing and the actual intent of the person. The most common safewords are red and yellow. Red means stop and yellow means to take it slowly. Dungeons and clubs may also have

their own choices of words. Safewords can be used to terminate the consent any time during the play.

2. DMs. Dungeon monitors also take the role of a bouncer in a BDSM club. They are meant to oversee the safety of the practitioners by keeping check safety standards of both the consent and the dungeon rules.

3. Basic knowledge. Practitioners are also encouraged to learn basic information related to anatomy, psychology and physics. For example, the neck is particularly vulnerable to damage and endorphin crushes can cause illnesses. Toys and their instructions on how to use must also be understood prior to a play.

4. Panic snaps. The more complex BDSM equipment come equipped with panic snaps. These are devices that can be operated with the use of one hand alone to free or disengage the device that restrains the person.

Chapter Seven: FAQ

Since dominance and submission are not part of mainstream sexual practices, it suffers from several misconceptions. It is also difficult to correct these myths because most culture still perceives it as a taboo topic. Portrayals in popular culture also add to the erroneous perceptions about the practice. Some of the FAQs about D&S are:

1. Do I have D&S tendencies? Some people think that only D&S practitioners take pleasure in the art. In fact, most studies show that each person will have a sexual fantasy that involves certain characteristics of D&S play. They may not necessarily be full-blown but only on a lower but still present in the BDSM scale.

2. I am a man but can I be a sub? Although majority of Doms are indeed men, there are still cases of men being subs and women being Dommes. This myth is also disproved with the existence of switches; persons can be both Doms and subs. This also disproves the myth that D&S are particularly abusive to women or that it is sexist.

3. Is D&S dangerous? Risk is definitely involved in the plays. However, various safety precautions both made by the parties involved and the dungeon masters are in place.

4. Is D&S a fetish? By the definition of a fetish as something that is used as a substitute for actual sex as a source of sexual gratification, domination and submission is not a fetish. It is instead an overall erotic behavior and lifestyle.

5. Is D&S all about sex? Some plays actually involve sexual intercourse however there are still some plays that only involve erotic practices that cause arousal and orgasm but without any physical contact. D&S arouses the more mental instead of the physical aspects of a person.

6. Are practitioners abusive? This is a word commonly associated with D&S because of the imagery it provides. However, the relationship is far from abusive. Pre-play preparations are done so that everything is consensual. In fact, the BDSM community encourages consent through the clear negotiation of boundaries which they say is more present in BDSM than in vanilla relationships.

7. Are Doms always abusive and subs will always have low self worth? This can be true for some but not all cases. In fact, most subs are actually in real life situations controlling and assertive people. They take pleasure and receive relaxation in the temporary surrender of their control. Doms too can also have traits similar to subs in real life situations and they take pleasure in the change of roles.

8. Is pain always involved? Another commonly associated word with D&S. There is indeed pain involved in some but not all plays. Some participants, who take pleasure in receiving, giving or observing pain, do indeed engage in plays involving pain. However, there is an entire set of plays that do not include pain.

9. Are tops always Doms and bottoms always subs? These pairings are not necessarily true. A top is the doer and the bottom is the receiver. A Dom can order a sub to top him. A sub can be ordered to top a Dom.

Conclusion

The world of dominance and submission is an alternative sexual lifestyle. Although the portrayals of the art are often the cause of misconceptions and misinterpretations, they have served their purpose by increasing mainstream awareness and also pique the interest of the public.

I hope this book did more than satisfy your curiosity for the art, I hope it has opened your mind towards this lifestyle. In the end, dominance and submission is not only about power but also about choice. The art may or may not be for you but if there is a soft whisper or a loud nagging in your innermost desires, know that art is inclusive to everybody.

Whether it is a secret fetish or a hardcore fantasy, the community is more than welcoming. Consider sharing your preferences to your partner, educating yourself beyond the information given in this book and start exploring the fulfillment of your desires.

After reading this book, experience will take over as your teacher. This book is only meant to provide you with information. You may use this information towards making your own decision that is right and appropriate for you.

Please Look For My Other Books

Below you'll find some of my other popular books that are popular on Amazon and Kindle as well. Simply click on the links below to check them out.

http://www.amazon.com/dp/B00WONC5AE

If the links do not work, for whatever reason, you can simply search for these titles on the Amazon website to find them. As always, a review is much appreciated and has a great impact on the direction of future books and storylines.

Thank You